The Revolution Will Be Publicized

Joy Elan

The Revolution Will Be Publicized

By Joy Elan

Dedication

I dedicate this book to my mother, Jackie. She always encouraged me to speak my mind and to be a writer. She worked hard to afford creative writing lessons and helped me process my thoughts. May she continue to speak to me through my ideas.

Table of Contents

Introduction

This little book is a collection of articles that I published for three different blog sites. I cannot believe how I got started. Yes, I can. It was so easy. A friend on Facebook tagged my name on Broke Ass Stuart's post about needing contributors for his site. I sent an email saying that I was a writer, and although I wrote mostly poetry, my writing was not limited to that. He accepted my proposal and I already knew what I wanted to write about first.

The Dangers of Driving While Black and Deaf was a topic, since Philando Castile had just been murdered. Having a disability or a hearing disability and not being able to hear the police officer's commands, I wanted to talk about something that was rarely discussed. When the article was published a day before my 33rd birthday, I was so juiced. It received a lot of views and comments. Then I got to work on a few more articles that I had in mind.

Since I was an activist and used to have student loans, I wrote the next couple of pieces about those experiences. The voting topic was important because people seemed to get sidetracked and focused only on the presidential election in 2016. Therefore, I came up with *Voting Locally Is More Important Than Voting for President.* I liked using the Broke-Ass Stuart platform to raise awareness.

My next favorite article for his site was *Tech Workers Have the Nerve to Complain about Cost, Traffic, and the Homeless.* I am an Oakland native and I was tired of feeling pushed out. I was not going to be pushed out, and I wanted to be the voice for the natives who were working in Oakland and San Francisco, making things happen, despite long commutes and high cost of living. After years of researching and speaking on gentrification, I was fed up when I saw an article about a tech worker who made $160,000 a year, complaining about not being able to survive in the Bay Area! I was like, "There are people who make way less and they're in worse situations than the people who make $160,000." The article was one of the most viewed because it talked about the privileged people who could not get their way.

My final big article for Broke-Ass Stuart was when the Golden State Warriors finally had a jersey that said *The Town*. I expressed the same frustration as other long time Warriors' fans who were there for the team, way before they went to the finals in 2015. Oakland was finally being acknowledged as the Warriors' "home," and it was really late for the acknowledgement; especially to the fans who have supported them throughout the years.

Shortly after that article, I was approached by Dope Era Magazine to write pieces for them. Dope Era Magazine was for the culture, especially for urban Oakland. My editor was an activist and I could speak more bluntly about social justice issues on their site. I wrote a few articles but one article that caught attention was *Oakland Author Challenges Mayor Libby Schaaf with Poem*, which was about me performing a gentrification poem at a homeless fundraiser; which the mayor of Oakland was also speaking at. The poem that I performed was about the natives of Oakland and how the mayor encouraged gentrification. That was one of my proud moments of activism; and to be able to share what that night was like was empowering.

A week later after the fundraiser, there was an incident at Lake Merritt, where a White woman called the police on two Black men for barbecuing. I saw the Instagram video and asked if I could write about it. The woman who had filmed the incident, Michelle Dione, was my editor for Dope Era Magazine. That article broke the news on Panther Times and went viral. I was credited for breaking that story and KRON 4 news asked how they could get in touch with the people in the video. The rest was history. My article was cited in Newsweek, and as a writer that was a huge accomplishment. I have to add that being a contributor for Panther Times was a huge honor, because I have always admired the Black Panther Party and I respect their work in the community with their survival programs. To carry on the legacy in a way and write for them was like receiving an award for my writing.

I love writing, and though I do not have it in me to write a book, writing articles was still fulfilling for me. I did not have to write an essay or a big book to get my point across. I nailed so many points in such a short format that it was enough for me. I do not really trust digital media, as things can be destroyed online; so I wanted to publish my articles in a book so that there will be a hard copy of the things that I wrote. My goal is to provide people with a roadmap of information that can be useful. Whether it is about education and how to get around the educational system, or the history of Oakland's residents, they are there as documentation.

I hope you appreciate what I wrote and how it documents what was happening during the time that each piece was written.

https://brokeassstuart.com/author/joye/
http://www.dopeeramagazine.com/author/joy-elan/
https://panthertimes.com/author/joyelan2001/

The Dangers of Driving While Black And Deaf

Every morning, I put on my hearing aids to bring some clarity into my life. I can hear; just not well. When I do not wear my hearing aids, the people who are talking sound like they are mumbling to me. So, I wear them from the moment I wake up until it is time to go to sleep (they are uncomfortable to sleep in).

I drive to work and walk around with my group of students at my community center. I forget that I am a Black woman with a hearing disability until someone points it out. I wear my identity proudly; but what if my identity gets me in trouble one day?

Lately, with the increase of Blacks being gunned down by the police, I wonder how my interaction would go if I were to be stopped. This has been a reality of mine since the shooting of Oscar Grant, which happened in my city, about five minutes away from my home.

I am afraid that I have to really read the police officers' lips, let them know that I have a hearing disability, and that I will follow their instructions so that they will not think that I am being disobedient. My license and registration are current and I make sure of that to minimize that risk.

I talked to my Deaf/hard of hearing friends about how they tell the police that they are Deaf without the police thinking that they are reaching for a weapon (trying to communicate in sign language could be mistaken for anything, if people aren't aware) . They showed me a card that they kept in their wallet, that they handed on top of their license. I felt some relief in knowing that I could obtain one of those cards.

Still, I have one more issue. My skin color. Is my skin color a reason for them to harass me more? I have been pulled over by the police a few times but they were cool and gave me a ticket (yes, it is cool to get a ticket instead of tased or beaten). Well, at least I lived to see another day and I lost a few dollars that I would make again in no time. I have to deal with these issues every day when I go out of my house; and I constantly think of ways to prevent me from having a situation escalate.

These are the things I think about while White people get to say how beautiful the sky looks and not have a care in the world. I just want to get home every night and be like Ice Cube, "Today was a good day."

Published July 25, 2016
https://brokeassstuart.com/2016/07/25/the-dangers-of-driving-while-black-and-hearing-impaired/

Breaking Free From The American Pipe Dream

When a prospective employer looks at your resume during an interview and sees that you graduated from two prestigious universities, usually they are impressed. When they see that I graduated from UC Berkeley and Stanford University, I am usually asked, "When it is the big game, who do you root for?" Or, "Aren't you overqualified for this job?" I smile, roll my eyes in my head, and politely answer the questions. Sometimes I wonder if the White candidates or candidates of other races are asked those questions.

As for the, "aren't you overqualified for this job" question, I did not know that being overqualified would be such a huge deal. Sometimes I have answered back by saying, "My student loans don't care if I'm overqualified," as if to say, "I just need a job, regardless of if I have too much education for it." It has been nine years since I received my Master's from Stanford, and I am still not in my field of study. I have met other people who have Bachelor's and Master's degrees, and they are in professions such as grocery clerks or janitors because they need to pay their bills. Shoot, there a lot of us working two or three jobs to keep up with our student loan payments and take care of our households.

How many of you are like me, applying for any full time job with benefits because you want to be able to retire hopefully by sixty? I am waiting for those Baby Boomers to retire so I can hopefully assume their positions; if they do not reduce them to part-time, or positions that are almost full-time but no benefits. Ugh! The American Dream has become the American Nightmare. Whether we are stuck in a job that we cannot stand, struggling to pay bills on time, raising children and hardly being able to see them, that was not what we wanted in our future. I think that my generation was sold an American pipe dream.

I found an old letter that I wrote to myself in 10th grade where I asked myself five years later, "Do you go to UC Berkeley and are you with your boyfriend from high school?" I was so full of hope and now, I am so full of determination to bring my goals to life. Things have changed so much, but I am slowly getting there. I do not want my degrees to go to waste; so I went ahead and put them to use by pursuing my writing career. All those years of writing essays gave me an advantage in how to write under deadlines and to express myself. I see a lot of posts on social media about "Pursue your passion," or "Do what you love and you'll never have to work a day in your life again." I may not make a lot of money in writing or doing the work that I do in the community, but I am hella happy and I live my life on my own terms!

We are in the times of the new hustlers and entrepreneurs. People are tired of waiting to be told that they qualify for the job; so they make their own jobs by putting their skills and hobbies to use. I learned that the college degree did not make me special; I made the degree special. I may not be the CEO of a company, but my life belongs to me the moment I sign out at work. At least I do not have to answer emails or calls once my shift is over (unless I did something wrong at work, which is very rare). So, do not be trapped by the American "pipe dream." Break free from that idea of what success is supposed to look like. I learned that being happy and living carefree is as successful as you can be.

Published August 2, 2016

https://brokeassstuart.com/2016/08/02/breaking-free-from-the-american-pipe-dream/

Teaching Kids About Money In A Debit/Credit World

My daughter is going to the third grade and over the summer, I've been working with her on her math skills. Her second grade teacher gave students a math packet to work on and hand in on the first day of school to their new teacher. I appreciated her teacher for doing that, because children tend to forget some things during the summer. The packet consisted of word problems, which were great because that was my daughter's weakness.

Another thing we have been working on is money! I remember the last time I met with her teacher about her progress; her teacher said to show her how to use money in the store. I quickly responded with, "But I use my debit card." The teacher realized what I said and responded, "You're so right. I do too!"

My daughter knows the debit card so well, that she tells me to pay with it. When we used to play store, she would ask, "How do you want to pay, debit or credit?" That was what she was hearing the store clerks ask each customer. I had some cash in my wallet, so I showed her what actual dollars and cents looked like. She was not going to have a debit card for a long time, so she needed to understand how to handle cash and change.

Our children are learning the automatic way of doing things and they don't understand the old fashion way of doing it. I still use a checkbook, but I don't balance my checkbook; I simply look online to see how much money is left and if the checks have been cleared. We have direct deposits and other ways of getting money electronically. When do we really use cash? One time, the tooth fairy forgot to put money under my daughter's pillow, so she told me to check the mailbox for a check. Our children don't really have the concept of how we get money, other than we go to work, it's in a bank, and on a nice looking card. The green paper, and coins with presidents' faces on them, is starting to become foreign to them.

At my job, I take a group of students with disabilities to the store to practice life skills using money. My daughter started to tag along with me and I would carry cash for her so that she could learn how to count. If something came up to $1.49, I would give her $1.50 or $2.00 so that she could learn how much money to get back. If I gave her only $1.00, she had to learn what she could buy up to that amount. When we would come back from the store, I would give her a worksheet where she added up the things she bought, and then subtracted that from the money she had. For most children, they need a visual to understand why we do math a certain way. Doing worksheets doesn't mean they can apply it in the real world.

Since I've been doing this exercise with her, I actually like carrying cash (just $5 or $40). It's nice doing some things the old fashioned way. We have to remember that our phones and computers may not work, and we have to rely on the traditional way to get things done. I never thought I would sound like my mom when I say I like doing things the old way, but in this instance with finances and math, the old ways work every time. We have to condition ourselves to think and not rely on technology so much. Our children are the future and they can process things faster; but they need to understand that the old fashioned, basic way of doing things can be useful in the future.

Published August 2, 2016

https://brokeassstuart.com/2016/08/12/teaching-kids-about-money-in-a-debitcredit-world/

Voting Locally Is More Important Than Voting For President

In less than three months, the election will be here. With all the focus on who will become the next president of the United States, we have a bigger focus on the local elections. While the presidents speak about policies and Black Lives Matter, they do not have the power to influence our communities. If we want things to change, then it starts with the city council, mayor, school superintendent, district attorney and etc.

I read four reasons about how important local elections are, especially for California: money, education, public safety, and information. We determine how policies are set for us; and we can control taxes, education, jobs, and anything we need by getting out to vote.

Currently, Oakland has a mayor who has not done anything for the people of color who are being pushed out. While people say that the previous mayor was bad, at least she helped get funding for youth employment programs and helped keep community centers open. Oakland's current mayor failed to apply for grant funding to keep the youth employment programs going, and she has not really addressed the decline of low-income housing. The city council members have been speaking up for their districts and trying to make a positive impact in their communities. The residents have been attending city council meetings to voice their frustration, and now we will be able to vote on these issues to make an impact.

I am a resident of Oakland, and I have to know who is running for office; because I would not want someone in office who may want to cut jobs or close schools. I work with the youth in my city because it is important for me to be a part of the community. I am aware of the people running for offices; from local all the way to presidency. I may not know which measures to vote for, but I get posters from my union about who and what to vote for.

When you get your ballot book, that's your time to do research on the issues on the ballot. If you're not sure what kind of impact they will have, look them up or ask someone. If you are part of an organization, such as unions, churches, or community groups, then they should be able to tell you who they endorse. There is no reason why things can or cannot change if we vote. Change starts with us and in our communities. Protesting brings awareness, but it does not change anything. Voting is our voice and it has power. We must exercise our power!

Published August 19, 2016

https://brokeassstuart.com/2016/08/19/voting-locally-is-more-important-than-voting-for-president/

Time To Start Thinking About Taking Care Of Our Parents When They Retire

When we were younger, our parents had some type of talk with us, whether it was about sex or our plans after high school. Now that we're older, we're having "the talk" with them about their plans for when they retire. I've seen people retire and then return to work to pay for their health insurance or other expenses. My mom is looking forward to retiring from her job of thirty years as a bus operator and getting senior citizen discounts at restaurants; and I am worried if she'll be able to pay her mortgage and other expenses.

My mother isn't able to do the things she used to do because of her work injuries. I've asked her if there's some type of work that she's interested in doing, and she doesn't have a plan. I want her to work at doing something she enjoys, or something that comes naturally for her, like culinary or cutting hair. I don't want her to be at Walmart greeting people to make a little change. I mean, damn! You retire from one job to work another 15-20 years at another job to pay the bills.

I have been living with my mom since I was a baby. I don't make enough for an apartment in Oakland, and a studio isn't worth almost $1,000 a month. It didn't make sense to pay rent, when I could pay to live at home with my mother. I am blessed to have a close relationship with her and she helps me with my daughter. It's a win-win situation. With both of us kind of stuck financially, I support her and I am aware of what's going on with her; and vice versa.

There is a post that I've seen of a mother going through phases with her child. She takes care of the child, then the child grows older, and then the mother grows older and the child takes care of her. Some of us are beginning to take care of our parents due to dementia, illness, financial struggles, and so on. We have to know our parents backup plans so we'll know what to do if we have to take over. I know some parents don't like to discuss their finances with their children, but it doesn't hurt to secure their future on our own (having our own insurance policies for them, knowing their medical history, etc).

My mom and I are a team. She loves to say, "We're all we got!" She is right, because if we don't trust each other, then we can't take care of each other. I hate feeling like I'm the parent in this situation, but it's my responsibility to take care of her. As we get older, it's harder for us to see our parents getting older too. Instead of feeling restraint and like she's a burden, I want my mom to enjoy her life. When I was a kid, I promised her that I would be a celebrity and buy her a nice, big house. Well, I'm not a celebrity (like I want to be), and I can't buy her

a big house, but I'm definitely a woman of my word.
Whatever my mom decides to do when she retires, I'm
going to help take care of her.

Published August 19, 2016

https://brokeassstuart.com/2016/08/19/having-the-
retirement-talk-with-your-parents/

Black Panther Party 50th Anniversary: Where Do We Go From Here?

October 2016 was a month long celebration for the Black Panther Party's 50th anniversary. A lot of events happened in Oakland with <u>Life Is Living</u> festival at deFremery Park, Joyce Gordon Gallery, and the museum/gala at the Oakland Museum of California. At the Oakland Museum of California, they had conferences and a concert. Then, there was the concert/rally at Frank Ogawa Plaza, which had a host of Oakland hip-hop artists, such as Kev Choice, Nu Dekades, Money B & Young Hump of Digital Underground, Mistah Fab, and so many more.

I had a chance to enjoy most of the celebrations. The Life is Living Community Forum with Youth Speaks had a collection of the free breakfast program, African dance lessons, and there were concerts on different stages. On the main stage was The Coup, and Girl 6 (a collection of six female singers from the Bay Area for a Prince tribute) with Kev Choice. That event was free for the community and there were food trucks and vendors. It was a sunny day and people came together to be a part of the legacy that the Black Panther Party left behind. To be at deFremery Park, where the Black Panthers used to host community meetings, was a special place; and it seemed like people soaked in the positive vibes.

The <u>Black Panther Party 50th Anniversary Conference and Gala</u> was October 20th through the 23rd, and it was a big event at the Oakland Museum with former Black Panther members and conferences. It had a concert on Saturday, the 22nd at night, and some local artists rocked the stage, such as Kev Choice, Martin Luther, Khoree the Poet, and Digital Underground. Also, there was an exhibit at the museum about the Black Panther Party and that exhibit is open until February 12th (information about the <u>Oakland Museum of California: Black Panther Party Exhibit</u>).

Black Panther Party 50th year Anniversary – Rally & Concert! at Frank Ogawa Plaza was a free event for people of all ages. It was hosted on Saturday, October 22nd too and the energy was electrifying. People of all ages and backgrounds were there and the message was that we have to take control of our communities. Hip-hop artists and activists used their platform to speak to the community and to share stories. Some of the DJs were: DJ Pam the Funkstress, Davey D, DJ Toure' of Hiero, DJ Tabu and DJ Julicio. The speakers were Mistah FAB, Cat Brooks, Shake Anderson, Minister Keith Muhammad, Mahmoud Abdul-Rauf (Retired NBA Star), Qubilah Shabazz (Daughter of Malcolm X) Saturu "James Mott" Ned (Black Panther Party), John Carlos of 1968 Olympics, and Zachary Norris.

Despite what people may say about the Black Panther Party, they were a group who believed in empowering their communities, and the things that they started are still being used to this day (free breakfast programs at schools, health clinics, free food programs, and a few others). Oakland was full of information and excitement. It was an honor to witness and be a part of a celebration of Oakland's own Black Panther Party. The message of where do we go from here was WE, the people, have the power to change things in our communities. Change starts with us. As June Jordan said, "We are the ones we have been waiting for." All power to the people!

Published November 19, 2016

https://brokeassstuart.com/2016/11/19/black-panther-party-50th-anniversary-celebrations/

References:

http://joycegordongallery.com/

https://www.bpp50th.com/

http://museumca.org/exhibit/all-power-people-black-panthers-50

http://www.pbs.org/independentlens/films/the-black-panthers-vanguard-of-the-revolution/

Self-Care Tips For All Year Around

This time of year can be hard for many people. Sometimes we're so busy helping others that we forget to take care of ourselves. I've learned how important self-care is, especially during difficult times like the holidays and recently with the not-my-president-elect. Here are some tips to help you in case you need a little reminding.

- ✓ Read a book
- ✓ Unplug from social media for a while (our minds can't handle all the negativity and drama online)
- ✓ Write (sometimes the best therapy is to get it out on paper)
- ✓ Listen to music (or play musical instruments)
- ✓ Treat yourself to a little massage or some form of pampering
- ✓ Exercise or walk: do an activity that makes you feel good physically, even if it's sex (wink)
- ✓ Cook and eat good food (drink some wine or beer too, but don't overdo it)
- ✓ Get a good night sleep (get off electronic devices an hour before you go to bed)
- ✓ Netflix and chill solo (go ahead and enjoy shows that are relaxing for you without having to entertain someone else)
- ✓ Garden
- ✓ Surround yourself with people who are positive and supportive (even if it means distancing

> yourself from toxic people who are family or
> friends)
> ✓ Take a mini road trip to another city and explore

I know I forgot some other things but I'm sure you can think of things that you enjoy doing alone. Read books to change your way of thinking and improve your quality of life, because those tools help us for the rest of our lives. We don't have to be rich financially; but we need to be rich mentally and physically. I'm a single mom, and my daughter asks to stay home because she's tired of getting up and running during the week. When we are at home, we do our own thing. She's in 3rd grade, so she enjoys reading books or playing with her dolls. So, children needs self-care as much as adults do.

Take a break from the world to protect your sanity. It's okay to stay home in your funky pajamas on a Saturday or Sunday, especially when all you do is get up and go to work every day. Or, doing something for yourself as little as thirty minutes to an hour, can impact the way you feel every day. Work towards your dreams. Give yourself something to look forward to before you jump out of bed for a busy day. Make a list of goals you want to accomplish so that you can have some guidance. Once you master self-care, it becomes easier. You may be alone, but you won't be lonely or bored. That's self-love; and you'll feel a lot better when you have taken time out for yourself.

Published November 29, 2016

https://brokeassstuart.com/2016/11/29/self-care-tips-for-all-year-around/

United, We Stand In Oakland (A Quick Reflection)

The Women's March in Oakland sent out a strong message. We *do not* support Trump, but we *do* support each other. As many as 60,000-80,000 people showed up to march around Lake Merritt and up to City Hall at Frank Ogawa Plaza. The march started around 10:30 or 11 am, and the performances at City Hall started around 1 pm. I did not march since I had to perform, but I drove by to see the power of people standing up and marching.

Some of the speakers and performers were: Project Bandaloop, Elaine Brown (community activist), Melanie Demore, Gayle McLaughlin (former Mayor of Richmond), DJ Nista, Lupe Rodriguez of Planned Parenthood, Moina Shaiq (founder of Meet a Muslim), State Senator Nancy Skinner, Tom Steyer (CEO of NextGen), and Mayor Schaaf (Info for Women's March In Oakland).

I performed my signature poem, I'm A Survivor, which was written in 2012 for the re-election of President Obama. The message of the poem was about being a Black woman in America from the Trans-Atlantic slave trade up until the present moment; and how she resisted with the different movements. The poem will always be relevant as long as there is oppression and resistance, and it was the perfect one to share. While I

was onstage looking out at the audience, I loved seeing
so many people gathering together to stand up for
what's right. I got chills and I fed off the audience's
energy. There were women, men, children, disabled,
interpreters for the Deaf, politicians, musicians,
teachers, students, and so much more. There were not
any arrests made and we shined yesterday.

The revolution was definitely televised yesterday. Now
that the marches are over, what do we do next? With all
this excitement and pictures about the marches and
what they represent, I hope people will carry this with
them and be about it. Do not say we are about support,
when the next day you will not help your fellow sister
or brother. It is not a women's thing, but a human thing!
We are all connected so let's be about that. We the
people are the change!

Published January 22, 2017

https://brokeassstuart.com/2017/01/22/106202/

https://brokeassstuart.com/author/joye/

Advocating For Parents In Special Education

Parents, what do we do when we learn that our child/children has a learning disability? In some ways, we want to deny it and say that they are being labeled for having too much energy; or maybe they prefer a specific subject more than others. Disability is a broad term for anything that is considered not the norm. Well, I have a different approach with that word. I like to use the term *different ability;* because we all are different, especially when it comes to learning.

If you have a child in special education, the first thing you must know is that you (the parent/parents) are in control of what kind of accommodation your child gets. This is set up by an Individualized Education Program or IEP. The IEP according to the California Department of Education is "Each public school child who receives special education and related services must have an Individualized Education Program (IEP). Each IEP must be designed for one student and must be a truly *individualized* document. The IEP creates an opportunity for teachers, parents, school administrators, related services personnel, and students (when appropriate) to work together to improve educational results for children with disabilities. The IEP is the cornerstone of a quality education for each child with a disability."

We must be proactive in researching resources for our children, so that when we meet with the educators, we know what to ask for. Many times, our children fall through the cracks because we did not know what to ask for or how to get it. You work as a team! It is not "you vs them." Everyone works together because we spend most of the time with our children, not the teachers. You have to know how to work with them at home, and everyone should be consistent. If the teachers see that you are very involved, and there is a plan in place, then it is about making progress and seeing what works best for the child. If you disagree with the educators' conclusions about your child's disability, then it is okay to have your child assessed by another therapist or doctor. You can ask your child's pediatrician for a referral of agencies that help examine children who may have a disability. In the San Francisco Bay Area, there are agencies that work with people with disabilities, such as Regional Center of the East Bay, Ed Roberts Campus, etc.

I know some children who were labeled as being on the spectrum for autism, and even when the parents disagreed with the label, they used it to get all the services that were designed to help their children. Suppose your child has a form of learning disability where they get speech therapy and pulled out for reading or other skills that need improvement. If the child is assessed on having a severe learning disability, then the disability is changed to that in the

IEP. When that happens, they can receive all kinds of services that is related to that disability and get more than speech and academic support. They can get extra time on exams, visual support, and other support that would not have been offered due to what the child was previously labeled.

This is when parents can say, "I want this, this, and this" for my child, and it has to be provided if it is documented in the IEP. After that, the ball is in the school's court. That is a legal document, and if it is not provided, the school can be held liable. Parents, you are in charge of this. Not the principal, not the teachers, or therapists. YOU! Do not let them give you the minimum. You tell them you want the maximum. I am telling you this as an educator, as a parent, and as a former student who had an IEP. The IEP is only for K-12 and it is not forever. It is confidential and it is only for school purposes (it does not have to be known outside of your immediate family). You want to ensure that your child gets proper support in education.

Having a disability is not a bad thing when you know how to help them be self-sufficient. There are many successful people who have a disability and many can overcome it when they learn how to use it. I have a hearing disability, but I know American Sign Language, and I got interpreters and other accommodations at school once I learned that they were available. I can only speak of the San Francisco Bay Area since I have been involved in disability rights and accessibility for a long time. Parents, especially parents of color, you are in control of your child's education. If you are truly concerned, do not be afraid to ask for help because there are places and people who can help you. Now, we have the technology and knowledge that was not available 20-30 years ago. Do everything you can to get your child equal access to a quality education.

Published February 2, 2017

https://brokeassstuart.com/2017/02/02/power-to-the-parents-in-special-education/

References:

https://www.rceb.org/

https://www.edrobertscampus.org/

Tech Workers Have The Nerve To Complain About Cost, Traffic, And The Homeless

There has been a lot of division between beliefs and lifestyles in the Bay Area. This is not regarding political parties; this is about regular working people and tech workers. The two worlds that have been colliding are becoming almost similar, once the tech workers started complaining about the cost of living in San Francisco.

Not too long ago, the tech industry complained about homeless people, and made fun of non-tech workers for not being able to live their wealthy, privileged lifestyles. They looked down on people who did not have successful careers and felt that they should not have to see homeless people on their streets. The "us" vs. "them" mentality really became aggressive when they were using technology to get ahead of other people. In the Mission District, they created an app to reserve public parks and told the natives to get off their reserved spot. When the natives refused to back down, it created tension between long term Mission residents and the Dropbox employees. Another sense of entitlement, was how they had private shuttles to and from their workplace, the luxury to work when it suited them, and the perks of getting free meals and technology; while the rest of us had to pay for these things.

The natives and middle class people in professions such as, teachers and fire fighters, were muscled out because of the high cost of living. Once they were gone, the tech workers were paying $1,000+ for renting a closet to have privacy in a room with 4-5 other people sleeping in bunk beds! In the SF Gate, a techie who made $160,000 a year, complained that he was not making ends meet living in San Francisco. They are living paycheck to paycheck to survive and learning what it is like for the rest of us. With all the money they are making, they still cannot afford to buy a home in the Bay Area; since the homes are going for over a million dollars. People are not homeless because they party, drink, and/or do drugs; they simply do not make enough to live in the Bay Area, even with two or three jobs, and multiple earners in the homes.

In The Guardian, it stated: "For their part, many well-paid tech workers complaining about their own predicament, say they also sympathize with the plight of people on more ordinary incomes. We think a lot about how people with normal jobs afford to live here," said the Canadian IT specialist. "The answer is: they don't. They commute from farther and farther afield." The digital marketer added: "During the first dotcom boom, we had secretaries commuting three hours into work … It's happening again. It was absurd then and it's absurd now," she said, adding that she and her husband both "know what it's like to be poor". Some tech workers expressed a sense of guilt about their complaints when so many people were worse off, including San Francisco's desperate homeless population."

This tech privilege came at a price; and they were really paying for it. How ironic is it that they may need to get on the affordable housing list? They may sympathize with the people who are not in tech, but the low-income and middle class people who are really struggling do not sympathize with the tech workers. Non-techs have been fighting this problem and their cries have been falling on deaf ears. Everyone works hard to survive in the Bay Area; but when you have people making four times your salary complaining, it's like, "Shut up! You don't know what it's like to really struggle!" The tech workers' side is really not that much greener. Their bubble is being popped, and they are learning what the world is really like.

Published March 16, 2017

https://brokeassstuart.com/2017/03/16/tech-workers-cant-make-ends-meet-in-san-francisco/

References:

https://www.theguardian.com/technology/2016/feb/17/san-francisco-tech-open-letter-i-dont-want-to-see-homeless-riff-raff

http://www.newsweek.com/san-francisco-tech-industry-gentrification-documentary-378628

http://www.sfexaminer.com/lets-honest-tech-industry-privilege/

https://www.sfgate.com/news/article/SF-techie-scrapes-by-on-160-000-salary-10966064.php

https://www.theguardian.com/technology/2017/feb/27/silicon-aa-cost-of-living-crisis-has-americas-highest-paid-feeling-poor

Hometown Hero Kev Choice Will Be At Yoshi's on June 30th

There is a musician from Oakland who has been rocking stages around the world for years. He plays the piano, raps, and produces; just to name a few of his many talents. You may have heard of him. His name is Kev Choice. He has released four albums and tours all over the globe. His music speaks about social issues happening in the Bay Area and around the world and his jazz flavor gives you a break from the noise happening around you. According to his bio, "being able to read and play music gives Choice an advantage over average emcees and producers.. 'I can communicate my musical ideas in multiple ways… I can take a beat that I make, and write it out for a band or an orchestra, or any configuration of instruments,'" (<u>Kev Choice</u>).

His musical resume is very impressive. He was Lauryn Hill's musical director in 2007. He has performed with some of Oakland's artists, such as, Too $hort, Mistah FAB, Goapele, The Coup, and Souls of Mischief. When he is not composing and performing, he is teaching at Oakland School for the Arts and being an activist in the community, especially at 51Oakland, which is a non-profit for providing art and music programs in Oakland Public Schools.

If you have not seen him before, you are in for a treat. He is performing at Yoshi's in Oakland on Friday, June

30th. He has performed there many times, and his shows sell out because he brings the musical originality and positivity that is really missing in modern hip-hop! I enjoy watching and listening to him in this intimate setting (videos of his music can be seen on YouTube). Tickets can be purchased at Kev Choice at Yoshi's.

He says, "Performing live is a way to take people on a journey. I want people to feel highs and lows, experience emotions, and relate to the things I'm saying in the music. I want people to see the amazing musicians in my band play at a high level and have us touch them with our musical gifts individually as well as collectively. I definitely always look to reflect my diverse musical influences in a show. I try to combine classical, jazz, soul, funk, rock, drum & bass, electro, and all types of music, in a Hip-Hop context. I like to stay current with my show, constantly adding new elements, trying new things, and trying to take it to a higher level." (Kev Choice)

Published June 7, 2017

https://brokeassstuart.com/2017/06/07/hometown-hero-kev-choice-will-yoshis-june-30th/

References:

https://kevchoice.wordpress.com/about/
https://51oakland.org/
https://www.yoshis.com/

The Dire Need For Vocational Classes In High Schools

There are many people with degrees who are not working in their field, drowning in student loans, and trying to survive. Are we in the age where a college education is becoming somewhat obsolete? I find people taking vocational/trade courses because they know that we will always need a plumber, mechanic, barber/hair dresser, electrician, carpenter, and so many more. There has not been a vocational course in high school in California since probably the late 1980s or early 1990s, when high schools began to focus more on the college track.

"States like California initially shifted away from vocational education in high schools in order to prepare students to enter the state's public universities," Forbes reported. Another reason vocational education has declined in California high schools over the last several decades, according to the Los Angeles Times, "is that a combination of overcrowding and budget cuts forced schools to convert shop rooms into classrooms." (High School Vocational Education On The Upswing, Coaxing Students Away From Traditional Colleges).

Now, California, and most likely other states in the country, are oversaturated with college educated people in minimum wage employment, waiting to advance at a company; which probably will never happen. If there were more people with trade skills, then there would most likely be more entrepreneurship and jobs to boost the economy in America. Currently, there are at least forty-three jobs that do not require college education, that pay very well – especially in technology.

There must be a reform in education that brings back vocational classes for people who are not going to college. Historically, many people have benefitted from these courses in high school, and then became employed right after graduating; allowing them to ultimately advance within their field. Vocational training in school would bring jobs back to the US, because people will have the skills to build cars, computers, or whatever the current demand is.

Right now, people are losing important skills listening to a teachers lecture about history or algebra, which will not be used in their professional career, unless they go into fields specifically requiring them. This article from the Huffington Post in 2013 regarding the state of Texas mentions, "The non-college prep track would be used to target students at risk of dropping out, according to the Paisano, the student newspaper at University of Texas San Antonio." Having vocational courses could prevent drop outs, and motivate students to look forward to life after high school. It will give them a sense of purpose and tools for survival.

NBC Bay Area wrote about this in 2010. "Indeed, California should acknowledge that it is quite possible for students to enjoy productive lives and successful careers without college, as several well-known state residents have proven. Why shouldn't California high schools offer career prep coursework for aspiring entrepreneurs like [Steve] Jobs, actors like [Hilary] Swank, chefs like [Wolfgang] Puck and models like [Gisele] Bundchen? Or how about instruction in other fields and industries that do not necessarily require a college diploma; such as automotive services, computers and information technology, home building, hotel and restaurant management, and sports and entertainment? The 100,000 or so youngsters who drop out of California high schools year by year represent unrealized potential. Many, if not most, could be encouraged to stay in school and to earn a diploma if they had the option of taking classes that prepared them not for college, but for a vocation."

Not only has California been losing students, which leads to more school closures, but they have been losing teachers because it is becoming harder to replace those who can teach college prep courses. If the education system re-implemented vocational courses, there could be an increase in demand for vocational teachers; because the ones who used to teach are retiring or have retired. More importantly, there would have to be a way around the requirements of teaching credentials to teach these classes, because it is about certification and experience in these fields. If someone has certification and years of experience as a plumber, mechanic, etc, that should be enough for someone to become a teacher without taking the unnecessary tests and going through the bureaucracy of teaching certification programs. Vocational training in high school needs to be re-emphasized; because not everyone's path leads to college.

Published July 28, 2017

https://brokeassstuart.com/2017/07/28/lets-go-back-to-the-old-school-the-need-of-vocational-classes-in-high-schools/

References:

https://www.forbes.com/sites/tarabrown/2012/05/30/the-death-of-shop-class-and-americas-high-skilled-workforce/#158a03fb541f

http://articles.latimes.com/2012/oct/28/local/la-me-auto-shop-20121028

https://www.huffingtonpost.com/2013/03/18/high-school-vocational-education_n_2900169.html

https://www.trade-schools.net/articles/trade-school-jobs.asp

https://www.nbcbayarea.com/blogs/prop-zero/Vocational-Training-Should-Be-an-Option-for-California-High-School-Students--99959039.html#ixzz4nJo7Uqub

The Evolution of Art & Soul

August 19th and 20th was the 17th annual Art & Soul Festival in Oakland. I had not attended one in a few years, and it was nice to get out and enjoy the music, performances, food, and most of all, the community.

Before there was Art & Soul, there was the Festival at the Lake (Lake Merritt), which occurred from 1982 to 1997 every Memorial Day Weekend. The Festival at the Lake was a family oriented event, with the same concept of Art & Soul. "Festival at the Lake is the city's chance to show off its array of cultural gifts." I grew up with the Festival at the Lake. It was the place that showed Oakland's diversity; and it brought different cultures and age groups together. It was where I ate food from different cultures and saw different groups perform. There were cool activities for the kids, like the fire department showing off their trucks and watching kids dance and sing. "There was a time, before public perception changed, when the fair was considered one of Oakland's cultural jewels. Billed as a multicultural extravaganza, it was an opportunity to explore, to share, and to appreciate the city's different races, along with their different foods, music and customs" (SF Gate Article in November 1997).

The event was so popular that over time, the neighbors complained about the traffic, and it began targeting specific groups of people. One of the things that changed the atmosphere was the presence of police and their interaction with the younger crowd in 1994. Despite them trying to be more inclusive with the younger crowd and getting their feedback, it changed the dynamics of the community. The attendance decreased, and after struggling to keep it sustaining, Memorial Day of 1997 was the final Festival at the Lake (SF Gate Article in November 1997).

In 2001, the first Art & Soul Festival appeared. Even though we had not seen anything like it for a few years, we recognized it and appreciated its evolution from Festival at the Lake. Art & Soul is literally blocked in from 14th and Broadway to 11th and Jefferson; that's quite a few city blocks to check out different stages and vendors. It is also very accessible to Bart and public transportation, making it easier to navigate. The event included different vendors selling artwork, books, clothes, jewelry, etc. The <u>food</u> provided had some of everything, from lumpia, jambalaya and Creole cuisine, Ethiopian, soul food, and other cultural foods.

There were different stages for specific performers. There was a Turf Battle, and Kida The Great was there (he is a successful teen dancer and choreographer from Sacramento, who has danced with Usher and other hip hop singers). Some of the main performers on Saturday were Oakland's own Adrian Marcel, Los Rakas, and headliner, Goapele. I was able to see all of this for $12! Everyone put on a great show. There was something else that was really cool too; there were two

American Sign Language interpreters there to interpret the lyrics (yes, Deaf/hard of hearing people like music too; but that is another topic). I did not attend Sunday's show; but the lineup on the main stage was still great, with Sydney Nycole, Lakeside, and Angie Stone.

When I walked around in between acts, I saw so many people there, including Oakland council members with their families; and the community was very engaging. Another cool thing was, I met another Broke-Ass Stuart writer there, Jamal Robinson, and we took an "us-ie." He came with his family, and it was like meeting a cousin at a family reunion; which is the point of the event. Based off of the pictures on Instagram and Facebook on my timeline, everyone had a great time, and it was like our farewell to the summer celebration. I am looking forward to next year's event and seeing the community out in the open again.

Published August 24, 2017

https://brokeassstuart.com/2017/08/24/evolution-art-soul-festival/

References:

https://www.artandsouloakland.com/
https://www.sfgate.com/bayarea/article/Oakland-Festival-at-Lake-mellows-with-the-times-3143781.php
https://www.sfgate.com/news/article/Festival-At-the-Lake-Discontinued-Debt-from-2796861.php
https://brokeassstuart.com/blog/author/jamalr/

The Town Warriors: A Letter From An Oakland Fan

The Warriors have decided to finally represent Oakland on their jersey, the city that they have been playing in since 1971. I am not going to lie, it feels kind of late to get the acknowledgement that they are Oakland's team, and have been for the last forty-six years. It is almost like we were the kids they never wanted to claim, but had no choice once the paternity results came back on national TV. "Warriors, you are Oakland's team!" When they were at their worst, the fans showed up and supported the team. I remember when tickets were cheap, like $20-$25 (someone mentioned tickets were $5 back in the day). Actually, it was not that long ago that the tickets were cheap either. Since 2014-2015's season, the ticket prices soared, even outside of the reach of the long term fans, who were mostly blue collar workers like the true Raiders' fans. The Warriors have always given back to Oakland, such as the Chris Mullins' basketball court at City of Oakland's Arroyo Viejo Park, and other community events.

The new team logo, which says *The Town*, has the Oakland tree as seen on the street signs in Oakland. This tree is not to be confused with Oaklandish's logo, which has a similar design. This is the City of Oakland's tree on the jersey. The Oakland fans fought hard to be recognized as Oakland, not San Francisco Bay. We got tired of the NBA showing the Oracle Arena and not mentioning Oakland. I guess the team helped the broadcasters to say what city is the team's home court. Although I am happy to see the new logo, a part of me feels like it was a smooth way to break up with Oakland. Oakland embraced the Warriors regardless of what the NBA called us because we know who they are. They are in East Oakland, right next to the Raiders and A's. They put the W in RAW (Raiders, Athletics, Warriors)! We are sad to see them go because we have come a long way and it is the end of an era. Warriors, thank you for finally acknowledging us after forty-six years. Here is to two more seasons; and as Al Davis of the Raiders used to say, "Just win, baby!"

Published September 25, 2017

https://brokeassstuart.com/2017/09/25/after-46-yearsthe-warriors-finally-acknowledge-they-play-in-oakland/

References:

http://brokeassstuart.com/blog/2015/06/09/the-warriors-belong-to-us/

http://www.nba.com/warriors/news/chris_mullin_basketball_courts_042312.html

High Career Aspirations Are Overrated, Here's Why

At this point in my life, I honestly thought I would be higher up on the career ladder; but I'm not. I am higher than the positions I used to be in, but I'm not high enough. And quite honestly, I'm okay with that. Let me back up for a second. In the last thirteen years since I graduated from college, I've been an aide in the classroom, a recreation center assistant, and a part time community college instructor. None of these jobs were full time and most of them, I was working two jobs at 45-55 hours a week, trying to make a full time living wage.

I got tired of running from one job to another while being a mother. Education became harder to get into unless it was a classified position; and even then I would have to find a summer job to pay the bills for the months that I was off. I had to step back and think outside of the box for a permanent job. What kind of jobs could I get with my degrees, where I wouldn't have to worry about technology possibly taking my job? I've always worked in service, because human support is still needed, and I love to be around people.

After applying to different positions for over a year, I landed a job as an administrative assistant. Finally, I have one job that is forty hours a week with benefits, and pays more than when I worked two jobs combined. I used to hate being in an office; but as I've gotten older, I knew that I needed to sit down all day to get more pay. I'm satisfied with what I do; I actually love it. The thing is, they asked me, "Where do I see myself in five years?" I said that I hope to move up to another position in five years. That was months ago at the interview, and now that I'm inside, I have a different perspective.

High career aspirations don't excite me as much, because the higher that I climb, the more responsibilities that I have; and there is no such thing as being off. When I come in on Monday mornings, I see that people answer emails and work on the weekends to finish by the deadlines. I thought that I had left that in college, and I'm not about that life right now. The higher pay may be nice; but what's your price for a peace of mind? It's priceless for me and I wouldn't trade anything for it. I think that I'll be in my position for a while. I wouldn't say that I'm settling, but I'm not in a hurry and that's being realistic for me. I love that when I go to work, I have eight hours to get it done, and when I turn off the computer for the day, I'm done. My job keeps me busy, which makes the days go by faster, and I don't have anyone watching over me. My role in the company is just as important as the supervisors and project managers, because I keep the company running smoothly so they can accomplish their work. Some people are better behind the scenes than in the spotlight, and I realized that I'm better behind the scenes. I haven't had a job like that in a long time and I feel free.

Also, I want to enjoy my life and spend my spare time doing whatever I want to do, including writing for this site. It's fine to coast for a while and enjoy life while I'm young enough to do so. I have to do what's best for me; and for now, I've found my peace.

Published November 9, 2017

https://brokeassstuart.com/2017/11/09/high-career-aspirations-overrated-heres/

Preparing for College Despite Public School Challenges

In California, particularly in Oakland, the school district has been failing families and the children with lack of funding and potential school closures. There is another issue of the school to prison pipeline, where students of color are punished harshly at school, and led to be suspended or arrested at school as early as five years old. Most of us cannot help our children with their math homework because of Common Core, and some of us are fortunate that our children attend an after school program where they can get assistance. With different barriers that affect us differently, it makes it hard for us to challenge the system or find ways to educate our children successfully.

But did you know that there is a way around the public education system to get your children to college? Despite what the teachers may think of your children, you can get them on the college track for free, or with very little money. You can enroll a child at a community college if they are mature enough to do so. Think about it; when did your high school grades matter when you attended any college course? When you got to college, whether a community college or a university, you had to take a placement exam to see what you know. From that exam, the counselors were able to see what classes you matched for.

It is the same thing for students under eighteen years old. A student will have to take an assessment exam to see what classes they would need to work towards their Associate's degree. The students can take classes not offered at their schools, and get the right education to prepare them for college or a vocation. And in some cases, the classes they take can help them graduate high school faster. This program is called Dual Enrollment. For Peralta Community Colleges, if they are in elementary and middle schools, the courses are free if they are enrolled under eleven units (2-3 courses). They have steps to take; such as getting a signed permission form from the school principal. From the Peralta Colleges Admission Information, I was able to get this information.

Elementary & Middle School Students

The Elementary and Middle School Special Enrollment provides enrichment opportunities for elementary and middle school students who can benefit from college level instruction.

The Peralta Community College District (PCCD) may admit a limited number of elementary and middle school students who have exceptional ability, or who desire specialized or advanced training. Such admission must be with the recommendation of the principal and approval of the parent or guardian. **Please note that not all four Peralta Colleges offer this program, therefore contact/visit the Admissions and Records**

Office on campus prior completing the Admissions application and the Elementary and Middle School Special Enrollment form.

Elementary and middle school students enrolling in a college level course must meet assessment requirements. The student must follow all the regulations and policies of the college, including adhering to any prerequisite requirements.

Special part-time enrolled elementary/middle school students are exempt from paying the California Community College enrollment fees and all other fees. Elementary and middle school students may not enroll in more than one class per semester, except during the summer term.

High School Students

Beginning Fall 2016, students enrolled in **eleven units or less** will not be charged enrollment fees or any other college/district fees, **except AC Transit Easy Pass Fee**. The AC Transit Easy Pass Fee will be charged to students enrolled in **six units or more**.* Special admit full-time students will pay enrollment fees, AC Transit fee, Health Fee, Student Representation Fee, and Campus Center Use Fee. **High school students enrolled in more than 11.0 units are required to pay enrollment and all other mandatory fees (See the current Peralta Colleges class schedule for current health, campus use and transportation fees).**

The High School Special Enrollment is specifically designed to accelerate the academic or vocational career of high school students. Access to the Special Enrollment Program is **NOT** allowed for:

- ✓ Remedial work (any classes in any discipline that are not college level and cannot be applied to an associate degree or higher). Remedial course numbers are 250 or higher.
- ✓ Work to make up for failed high school or middle school classes.
- ✓ Recreation or hobbies.
- ✓ Any class that can be taken at the local high school.

Not many of us are aware of our choices and it is legal to do this process. I graduated from high school a semester early because I went to summer school at my high school every year to get ahead. When I graduated early, I went to a community college to get started on my college units. When I started my freshman year at UC Berkeley, I completed nine units, which was almost one semester. The summer break for college students is about three months. Instead of vacationing, I went to summer school for the first six weeks, then had the 2nd six weeks off. I went to summer school every year at UC Berkeley to take classes required to graduate. By the time fall started, I completed 6-8 units. I graduated from UC Berkeley in three years! A teen in Indiana got her Associate's degree then graduated with her Bachelor's degree right before she graduated from high school. In fact, she got her Bachelor's on May 5, 2017, then got her high school diploma a few weeks later on May 22, 2017.

 This is your chance as parents to change your children's lives and go around the education system. Summer school is not offered except to repeat classes because some schools did not want students to graduate early. They may have taken that option from us, but we can do something else to make our children productive. Also, at the community college, students can take vocational classes that are not offered at their school. Not everyone is meant to go to a university. You can be just as successful as a plumber, mechanic, beautician, chef, and so many more. Also, they can transfer these units to a four year college when they want, and it will reduce their student debt and units because they took the required general education courses needed for a Bachelor's degree. This is your chance for your child to discover what they are good at and get them ahead in the education game.

Published March 6, 2018

http://www.dopeeramagazine.com/2018/03/06/preparing-for-college-despite-public-school-challenges/

References:

http://web.peralta.edu/admissions/enrollment-steps/elementary-middle-school-students/

http://web.peralta.edu/admissions/enrollment-steps/high-school-students/

Eartha Kitt's Legacy in Organic Activism

Entertainment and activism have always gone hand in hand. People do not know the ripple effect of their actions with breaking down barriers until they are placed in those situations. When a person is trying to overcome something in their dreams or line of work, they are going to figure out a way to tear down the walls. They become activists and trailblazers only when they are confronted with the issues and are making too much noise tearing down those barriers.

Before Colin Kaepernick and Muhammad Ali, there was a trailblazing woman by the name of Eartha Kitt. Eartha Kitt is known for her role in the Batman series in the 1960s and her song, Santa Baby. She stood up because of her background as a biracial woman raised in the south. She was born in South Carolina on January 17, 1927, during a time when people still did not know that slavery had ended in 1865. Because Eartha was biracial, she was often stigmatized for being light-skinned, and that meant catching hell from the Blacks and Whites. When she moved to Harlem as a child and started taking dance lessons, it was then that she discovered her talents and passion for dancing. She went on to become a famous dancer and singer.

Even though she was successful in her singing and acting career, she protested with Sammy Davis Jr. against Las Vegas venues that they headlined at for segregated accommodations or second class access through the back door and kitchen. But none was more troubling than when the First Lady of the White House, Lady Bird Johnson, invited Eartha Kitt to her luncheon in 1968. The invitation asked the fifty attendees to bring ideas about the problems among the young people of America at that time. Lady Bird Johnson had other ideas that were not related to the theme, such as how the White House was doing and putting down flowers along Route 66. Kitt brought the attention back to the subject of the luncheon, and she spoke up about people not wanting to fight in the Vietnam War. Eartha Kitt was doing what she was requested to do, be the voice of the people and presenting it to the White House. She caught backlash immediately, as it had appeared that she had been blacklisted from performing at the same venues she previously sang and danced at on the regular.

Eartha was unapologetic for speaking up, as she did not see how it would be problematic to talk openly in a country that claims Freedom of Speech for all of its citizens. We have to remember the time-period of the incident was during the Civil Rights movement. Black people knew there was an unspoken, double standard rule, where they were not allowed to speak back to Whites (and she was not), let alone the President and the First Lady of the United States. The government made an example out of her and she was forced to move to Europe because she could not work in America.

"For years I went along with the idea that entertainers should not get involved with politics. Today, I realize that because of our contact with the public, we have to speak out, to make those who are responsible more aware of what is happening where they perhaps cannot see. Particularly someone like myself, who has lived the life of poverty," as stated by Eartha Kitt.

When Black entertainers or athletes spoke up about any social injustice, they became targeted by the CIA. Ossie Davis, Ruby Dee, and Harry Belafonte did not find themselves blacklisted as actors, but Eartha Kitt did. It appeared that the government picked and chose who they wanted to tear down if they spoke too truthfully about the Vietnam War.

History showed us of the 1968 Olympics with Tommie Smith and John Carlos raising a fist in the air, the dismantling of the Black Panther Party, and Muhammad Ali. The most recent and relatable event of our time now is how Colin Kaepernick has been verbally attacked by our current President Donald Trump for kneeling during the national anthem to protest police brutality. Now Kaepernick is facing a similar blacklisting from the NFL and sponsorships, to Eartha Kitt's sudden inability to find work after her honest remarks that day at Lady Bird's luncheon. Artists and entertainers who are first to break the social silence of a glaring problem, often experience the pain of social injustice. When they do something about it, they are told to be quiet and learn their place in society. What good is performing when they are still restricted in some ways in what they do and where to go? Kitt, as well as other entertainers during that time, left for Europe, where they did not have to worry about segregation, isolated from progress. Some returned to America years later, after the storm calmed down; but they still had to worry about the government watching them. The ironic thing was that Eartha Kitt never tried to be an activist. She merely stood for what she believed in and said what she felt needed to be said. Organic activism is not sought out, it is discovered within.

Published March 15, 2018

http://www.dopeeramagazine.com/2018/03/15/eartha-kitts-legacy-in-organic-activism/

Reference:

TV One's Unsung: Eartha Kitt

The North Pole is an Oakland Mini-Series About Gentrification Everyone Should Watch

No other show can share Oakland's story about gentrification like the web series, The North Pole. It touches on all of the social issues that Oakland natives are experiencing during these unsure times. The show focuses on three friends; Nina, Marcus, and Benny, who live in North Oakland, hence the term North Pole. They are the polar bears who are becoming extinct in their own environment, with fighting against rent increases, changes in the neighborhoods with newcomers, and jobs in the community, which do not reflect what Oakland is about.

The show's comedy brings relief, but it is also very informative. The metaphors of the North Pole resemble what is happening in the ecosystem and adaptation of natural habitats. There was a reference of the Pizzly Bear (part polar and grizzly), and how they are mating due to changes in environments. It sounds familiar with what is happening with diversity. The show is relatable and captures all of these issues in such a short time frame.

One episode that highlighted the complexities of gentrification was when Nina and Marcus took their White roommate to the suburbs for Marcus' family reunion. Marcus' brother and cousin, who was played by Mistah F.A.B. and W. Kamau Bell, were talking about how hard it was for them to live in the suburbs. Although they joked about trading a Range Rover for a Prius, that was a reality for people who commute from the suburbs to Oakland to work. The other issue was not being close to family members because everyone had to move out to where it was cheaper, whether it was Antioch, Vallejo, Stockton, etc. There was a deep line in the show, where Marcus' mother said, "The suburbs used to be the place where the rich folks wanted to live. Now, it's where the poor folks are forced to live."

The North Pole is one of these shows that tells contemporary stories and was actually filmed in North Oakland. You can see all of the highlights, such as Mosswood Park, Temescal district, and the casting was well done, with people who represent Oakland.

To view the episodes: go to The North Pole website at http://www.thenorthpoleshow.com/.

For each episode, there is information listed on how to get involved in different organizations.

Published March 20, 2018

http://www.dopeeramagazine.com/2018/03/20/the-north-pole-is-an-oakland-mini-series-about-gentrification-everyone-should-watch/

Reference:
https://youtu.be/drRPhlp1fxc

Oakland Author Challenges Mayor Libby Schaaf with Poem

A few days ago, I was invited to perform for a benefit that was raising money to house women with children and combat homelessness.

I performed a poem that speaks about gentrification called ***Old Oakland vs. New Oakland*** (the video is on YouTube), which touched on all the issues that were caused by gentrification.

Old Oakland vs. New Oakland was written in 2016, after reading numerous articles on how people were using Nextdoor to racial profile Black and Latino residents in Oakland. White residents were complaining about Black churches being too loud. The high cost of living forced people to move out of Oakland even though they worked in Oakland. Also, this was something that I was personally dealing with, and from observing other people on a daily basis.

I called the poem Old Oakland vs. New Oakland because in May 2015 at the 11th Annual Oakland Indie Awards, Oakland Mayor Libby Schaaf gave a speech in which she said, "Let's give it up to the new Oakland!"

I interpreted Schaaf's statement as if she did not want the old Oakland natives there anymore, and she was trying to get the new businesses and residents to take over. For example, when Schaaf helped Uber to occupy the "uptown" area of Oakland before they backed out of the Sears building after numerous scandals.

At the reception of the Oakland Indie Awards, Netta Brielle was performing, and she asked how many of us were from Oakland. Only three of us made some noise out of the few hundred people who were present. ***That was the first time I could see the full impact of gentrification in that space.***

My poem ended up being part of a short novel I wrote about Oakland natives trying to live and work in their community. It took place in 2015 when the Warriors won the championship and when some policies were changing the landscape of Oakland.

The book, *Holding On To My Pride*, is a sequel to my first novel, *Life Is A Canvas*. I wanted to share our stories while it was relevant. It still is because we are impacted by these policies every day with the increase in homeless encampments, and no long-term solution for affordable housing and improvement in pay for service workers.

Back to the event that happened a few days ago, I knew that my poem would speak to the people who were from Oakland, who most likely worked in or near Oakland and were forced to move out of Oakland.

The thing that made my performance significant was that Mayor Schaaf was there as a speaker and she was in the audience when I performed the poem. I was kind of nervous because I was not sure how it would be received; but I had a duty to share what we have been saying. I was talking about her to her face and quoting what she said at the Oakland Indie Awards. After I performed, a lot of people came up to me and told me that they appreciated me being the storyteller for what they were experiencing. Mayor Schaaf never approached me about the poem.

As a writer and spoken word artist, the audience's words meant a lot to me because my goal is to tell our stories and keep our history alive.

It is my duty to speak up and bring awareness to different social issues. I want to be remembered for standing up to the mayor on behalf of the natives of Oakland.

I am an artivist (artist and activist), and that night was one of the highlights of my writing and spoken word career. ***I may be Old Oakland, but I am letting New Oakland know that I am not leaving my city.***

Published April 24, 2018

http://www.dopeeramagazine.com/2018/04/24/oakland-author-challenges-mayor-libby-schaaf-with-poem/

White Privilege Used to Fight Racially Charged Harassment at Lake Merritt

Oakland, Cali – On a sunny Sunday morning at Lake Merritt, a couple of people wanted to have a get-together and enjoy the scenery. However, that pleasure was interrupted when a woman decided to show up at their spot and call the police.

It does not take much to figure out what color they were and what color she was. The guys are respected members of the community, and they were having a joyous moment. They had their spot, and no one seemed bothered; except this woman. She took it upon herself to call the police. It was discovered that she had been at the scene for two hours pretending to be on the phone with the police to intimidate them.

According to one of the men targeted, Kenzie Smith, the White lady was bothering him and his friend, Deacon for BBQing at Lake Merritt in a designated BBQ zone.

"I got out of the car at Cleveland Cascade stairs, and when I walked across the street, she was standing there on the phone. She said, 'Oh great, another nigger.'

Smith looked around because he didn't know who she was talking to. He was the only Black person in that area of the sidewalk. He walked over to his friend Deacon, where he had the BBQ, and said, "Yo bro, what's going on?"

He told Smith she had called the police for BBQing. "We both started cracking up, laughing," Smith said.

According to Smith, it was around this time when a young Black lady was standing over to the corner. She approached the table where the BBQ was being set up and introduced herself. She said she had witnessed the situation. By this time, the White lady walked over to the table, slammed her fist on it and said: "There's no BBQ today, you need to leave."

"She was saying things like, 'We weren't welcome in the area of the lake.' She told me and Deacon that she owned Lake Merritt. Also, she said we were not welcomed to be there. I felt like she was saying Blacks weren't welcome," Smith said.

Smith said, "She kept saying we were going to jail. She said that she was going to file a complaint for us cooking BBQ in the park. She said she knows her rights, that the rights state if she tells the police that she has a problem with us then we are going to go to jail."

This one experience is not anything new to Black Oakland residents who want to chill on the east side of Lake Merritt (the Lakeshore Avenue side). Lake Merritt is a public park, which does not require a permit. It is first come, first serve, as long as people are not doing anything illegal.

Davey D talked about this extensively on Facebook and was mentioned in the East Bay Express in May 2015, "Even when 'permitted events' took place, hostile residents living by the Lake organized and tried to shut them down if it was too many Black folks. Case in point, last 4th of July, several thousand dollars was laid out to have an annual 4th of July party and picnic.

Unbeknownst to organizers, a group of residents in the luxury high rise 1200 Lakeshore, held a series of meetings, including one with Park and Rec to get the event canceled.. What saved the day were the Black residents who lived there and pushed back…"

Cases like this go back to the Festival at the Lake, a long time Oakland event and tradition that shut down when White residents near the lake complained about the festival drawing the "wrong kind of crowd." Occurrences like these are when privilege shows up and manipulates laws to their advantage. It is okay to have a picnic, but not a BBQ. Same thing, different choice of words and demographics.

Smith said, "I was like, so if you tell the police that two Black men are BBQing, that means we're going to jail. I just didn't understand the logic in the situation. And then it was like, she would continuously say little things to us, and she would act like she was on the phone talking to the police. She would say things like 'Yea he's wearing this," or she would say, 'Yea, he won't look at me officer because he thinks he's going to jail.' Or she would say, 'Yea, he's going to be somebody's bitch in there.' It was mind-boggling the things she was saying."

Smith said, "It was like, if someone was to put you in a box and say all the hurtful things to you at one time. That's how it felt."

Smith's story continues as he mentioned that his friend Deacon, who was first at the scene had already been harassed by the woman for a while before Smith arrived. Deacon told Smith he did not know the woman, that she just came out of nowhere, called the police and kept telling him he had to leave.

According to Smith, when the young Black lady showed up (mentioned earlier), she was walking around the lake and heard what the lady was saying; heard it was racist. So she stopped to see what was going on and asked Deacon if everything was okay. She started filming and put that much of the incident up on her Facebook. Unfortunately, we were not able to get her contact information before she left.

The young woman asked the White lady to please move herself from the area. The White woman turned it back on her and told her to "mind her fucking business. This is my property. You don't even know what's going on." The White woman became more aggressive towards the young Black woman. "It just was weird. It was like, I think she wanted a reaction today. And she didn't get the reaction she was looking for," Smith said.

Smith had enough of the encounter with the White woman, for an hour he had dealt with her harassment. He decided to call his wife who was up the street, telling his friend Deacon, "You'll see what she does. Just watch."

Kenzie's wife, Michelle Dione, showed up around 12:50 pm. Dione walked up to the White woman, ready to film, as she had already been sent a picture of the lady and knew what she looked like.

Dione is a White woman and what was cool about this was she was using her privilege to stop it. Dione knew her rights, and she was not harassing the woman.

"There's this silent code of behavior that White women know; they are taught if you just change your tone you can often be deemed 'innocent' and believable to the point that your word becomes law. When I first approached her, she had that tone, the one that we are supposed to speak to police officers, the one that makes us automatically justified no matter what. I don't think she expected me to bypass her bs and call her out," Dione said.

The woman stole a business card out of Dione's hand, which started the second longer video Dione recorded. Dione said the woman tried to use her "victim voice," and used a lot of trigger words to get the police to be there faster, such as "they are threatening me" when it was just Dione who was confronting her in her face.

The White woman who was harassing wanted to make sure that the men and women at the park were held responsible for her authority as a White woman. However, the woman did not like that someone was watching her and following her. She got a taste of her own nasty, racist medicine. All she had to do was mind her business and stay away from the area.

After the lady ran away to a Quik Stop on Brooklyn and Newton, the police arrived and talked to her. The officer told Dione that she did not do anything wrong following her as long as she did not touch her. Dione informed the police that the woman should have called the Park services and not the police. The police agreed. As Smith noticed that she appeared to be mentally unstable, the police said that she wanted to evaluate her mental health too.

All this was taking place within 30 minutes, and despite the police showing up, the lady returned later at 4:15 pm according to Smith. The White woman harassed them again and said they weren't supposed to be there, they were supposed to move. Smith told her that the Oakland police officer said to them that they did not have to move, and that the charcoal code was not enforced.

Published May 2, 2018

https://panthertimes.com/2018/05/02/white-privilege-used-to-fight-racially-charged-harassment-at-lake-merritt/

References:

https://www.eastbayexpress.com/SevenDays/archives/2015/05/19/oakland-police-threaten-to-cite-residents-for-barbecues-by-lake-merritt

https://www.facebook.com/mrdaveyd/posts/10155530814045720

https://youtu.be/Fh9D_PUe7QI

Oakland Organizers Take Action After BBQ Harassment at Lake Merritt

A week after a video of a White woman harassing two Black men barbecuing at Lake Merritt for hours went viral the story has somewhat lost its narrative.

The two men involved, Kenzie Smith and Onsayo "Deacon" Abram, did not get a chance to share much of their side of the story to what happened before the filming of the woman.

The story went viral at the same time Urban Peace Movement and DNas had already organized 510 Day. 510 Day is an annual event that happens on May 10th (5-10). People from the Bay Area knew of 510 Day and used that to say "fuck you" to gentrification.

People outside of the Bay Area thought it was a cookout and us having a party to spite the White female harasser who we like to call the "Charcoal Police." Others on Twitter have been using the hashtag #BBQBecky.

510 Day is a day for Oakland natives to share our history about the Black Panther Party and other historical events that happened in Oakland. The lake was the perfect spot since it was a smaller version of Festival at the Lake.

However, 510 Day was taken out of context for those outside of the Bay Area and knew of Oakland's culture. It was a day for us to come together and celebrate, but we were also bringing awareness to the institutional racism in Oakland. That was not enough though.

Smith and Deacon had a chance to share their perspectives with iNeverWorry podcast hosted by DB Bedford, and you get to see what that day was like from them.

Smith is a godson of original Black Panther member Saturu Ned, and Deacon is an Oakland native. They grew up going to Lake Merritt for barbecues and parties and know how it used to be before new park laws put in place that now negatively affect Black residents from hanging out at Lake Merritt.

A rally called, "Grill Your Government," was organized on May 15 at city hall by Carroll Fife, to make demands for change in policies with the city of Oakland. Council member Brooks of District 6 was the only one who reached out to help organize the group to speak at city council.

Before going inside, the speakers rallied in front of city hall for different community members to talk about the effects of gentrification mixed with longtime Oakland residents who have had hidden racially charged motives, to put new Lake Merritt rules in place; such as "non-charcoal barbecue approved zones," which are not currently enforced.

Some of the speakers included Oakland mayoral candidate Cat Brooks, Oakland city council District 2 candidate Nikki Fortunato Bas, Laney College journalism student and filmer of the BBQ harassment Michelle Snider, Mike Hutchinson, and Samba Funk who used to drum at Lake Merritt. The purpose was to demand Oakland city council change the rules to benefit residents of all Oakland districts better.

This incident was without question racially motivated, considering the two men's collaborating stories, along with the video and a third witness who live-tweeted the entire event.

Many Oaklanders have been seeing an increase of cops called on Black people for doing normal activities and having fun. It is often a game of White privilege, exercised and abused in a show of power; and that was not going to be accepted by people who grew up in the community.

"They want us to follow the rules when they accommodate you, but you change the rules on the floor to suit you. We demand a formal investigation into the background of this woman who called the police regarding this possible contract work with the city," Fife said to the city council.

Fife also said there was a need for police protocol to determine how many city resources have been wasted by minor non-threatening response calls.

"We want this reconsideration by the council of the regulations that allowed this to happen, and that are imposed at Lake Merritt. And finally, we want a resolution from city council to impose fines on people who make baseless 911 calls and waste resources," Fife said just before leaving, as a group of protesters walked out with the speakers yelling out five times, "All power to the people!"

In closing, come join us at BBQ'in While Black at Lake Merritt on Sunday, May 20th from 11 am until we are done. Most importantly, if you're registered to vote in Oakland, pay attention to the June and November ballots. June is the state and county district elections, and we have to put in a new District Attorney, most likely Pamela Price. In November, Oakland is voting for a new mayor and new council-members for Districts 2, 4 and 6. Organizing and speaking at city council is exercising our power; but what is more powerful, is voting and getting rid of the people who are enabling gentrification.

Published May 17, 2018

https://panthertimes.com/2018/05/17/oakland-organizers-take-action-after-bbq-harassment-at-lake-merritt/

References:

https://urbanpeacemovement.org/

https://www.youtube.com/watch?v=IvMIoQ3vIrE

https://www.youtube.com/watch?v=fnilzzNUBME

https://www.ineverworry.com/

https://www.eastbayexpress.com/SevenDays/archives/2018
/05/01/oakland-elections-cat-brooks-jumps-in-mayors-race-
and-contests-for-two-council-seats-become-crowded

https://www.eastbayexpress.com/SevenDays/archives/2018
/02/01/nikki-bas-challenger-to-oakland-councilmember-
abel-guillen-raises-43k-in-two-months

https://www.youtube.com/watch?v=vcjNe_HslJA

https://mikehutchinsonforschoolboard.wordpress.com/bio/

http://sambafunk.com/

https://www.eastbayexpress.com/oakland/the-express-
2018-june-endorsements/Content?oid=16110772

https://www.eastbayexpress.com/oakland/a-bare-knuckle-
fight-for-top-cop/Content?oid=16110603

Raw Interview of Kenzie Smith Regarding Run for Oakland City Council District 2

Hey Kenzie, you've been really active in the community since April 29th. I've been following you and what you're trying to change in the community.

When Rebecca Kaplan nominated you for PRAC, what was the purpose of that? What does PRAC do?

"PRAC oversees the City of Oakland Parks and Recreation department and makes sure things are getting taken care of. Anyone can put in to be a part of it; but it helps when a city council member nominates you. That was what Rebecca Kaplan did for me."

What was the difference between 510 Day and BBQin While Black events at the Lake? "510 Day was already happening, and that was no association between me and Deacon. The organizer invited me to be a part of that since my incident had just happened a week before. BBQin While Black was hosted by Jhamel Robinson and Logan McWilliams. They wanted to collaborate with me, and I didn't want to be in the media, I just wanted to be behind the scenes. I cried when I got there and saw about 300 people setting up at 9:30 am. I was touched because people came in from out of town. I'm talking about Washington, Los Angeles, all over. I hadn't seen people since middle school and high school. The new one on July 1st has the theme of

Poetic Justice, because I will be having poets perform and people from the city council and PRAC. I want to showcase and bring people together. I want to use my light to shine on other people in the community. Whoever I rock with, I'll shine the light on them. I've always been in the background, never been a person on social media."

So what changed?

"I've been an activist since 2000, doing backpack drives with my bro, Mistah F.A.B. Then in 2016, I did a community give back, where we passed out hygiene kits, food, clothes, haircuts to the homeless. I had totally forgot I did that until Facebook brought back one of the memories, and I was like, "Oh yeah." But when I saw the pictures, I was like wow.

So many mothers showed up who said they couldn't afford school supplies and backpacks. Even toys. This is nothing new to me. I've been in the community, and I grew up in the days where you couldn't go to certain areas without knowing someone in that neighborhood. Now, we lost ourselves and our values. We have kids raising themselves. I saw a 12-year-old girl who was pregnant, and she told me that she was grown. I was like, [What the hell?] How is she grown? But we've got to do much better."

What you do inspires me and a lot of others. A lot of people don't know where to go; they always look for

leaders. And sometimes I'm like, "You have to be the leader." I love capturing your brother, Jhamel, you, everybody, really grass-rooting it. Whether people donate or not, you're like it's happening anyway.

I was inspired by my brother and my wife, Michelle to become more active. You have to learn to adapt or create your own ways. Sometimes I ask my brother what he thinks. My bro, Mistah F.A.B. was in South Africa, and he called me, and they were talking about it over there. I was worried that he didn't like the attention, but he was proud of me. He was telling people there that I was his brother and he was proud! He liked the way I used my brain in the situation. I didn't use my brawn. He said that we brought back Festival at the Lake. I've got to get out there and change things."

So now, what made you want to run for City Council?

"I was speaking at a fundraiser in San Francisco called Youth Awards. Some kids that were there came up to me and asked what can we do? I told them to vote, and they were like for who? They said if I run, they'll vote for me. That was a doubled edged sword for me to run, because I had the younger generation's attention. If this is what will get them out there to vote, then I have to run. It's not about winning or losing for me. It's about getting the younger people active in the political process."

Now, you've announced that you're running on June 25th, what's next on your itinerary for running? Fundraisers and stuff?

"Life has changed now that I've announced it. I have someone that stepped up to take care of the social media. Other people have stepped up, and I really thought I was going to be doing this by myself. They want to see me win. They want to see Oakland change. Like, I am still helping Drew get a place, but he needs an I.D. So, I've been busy working with a program that will help him and get him settled.

A couple of weeks ago, I did Hands Across the Lake. I've been in the community, I want to be accessible to people. I am always at the lake. I have no reason to run away from the people when it's the people who made me who I am. Whether it's Black, White, Purple, Blue, Yellow, Green, I accept everybody. I wanted to attend Pride, but I had a conflict. I want to thank the LGBT community for their support. As for the campaign, I want to do it by the book, be transparent."

We have some heavy hitters running for mayor and re-election that will help our community, like council member Desley Brooks (District 6)...

"Desley Brooks is the homie! She told me to tell the audience at the Juneteenth event at Arroyo Viejo Park that I was going to run. I was trying to chill that day, but she encouraged me to let the crowd know that I was there. She's very supportive, and she's not in my district. She has seen my growth and my grind and encouraged me."

I have a lot of respect for council member Brooks. She's always at community events in other districts, whereas I rarely see the other council members in districts outside of their own. She has done a lot for her district though. Which brings me to this: what are you trying to accomplish as a council member? What kind of impact do you want to make?

"I want; a better arena for the community to come together; whether it's a weekly event at Lake Merritt, or somewhere in the community.

Tackle the homeless issue. Since I've done my own work, I already know what works and doesn't work.

Help the non-profits since their funding keeps getting cut.

Work with schools to provide better after-school programs and childcare. These kids need someone to talk to, someone to guide them. I want to establish programs for youth.

Talk about teachers and increase their pay, and get them supplies in the classrooms. As a parent, I was fortunate to buy my daughter a graphing calculator that costs $150. But how many other parents can afford that?

I want to call out the mayor. I was at the celebrity baseball event, and she was sitting next to me. She wouldn't even acknowledge me, not even a hi. It's cool, because she showed me her true character. I only deal with people who deal with me. But back to her, she's the reason why we have the homeless crisis and it's too late for her to do anything. Cat Brooks supports me, and that's all that really matters."

Do you think we're sending a strong message that we are tired and we're going to beat them at their own game?

"I can't speak for them; but for me, things in the community needs to be addressed. It not always about being a hero or the bad guy. Have you seen The Avengers with Thanos? Thanos was making people disappear. Well, Blacks are disappearing, Asians are disappearing, Mexicans are disappearing, but the Whites are appearing. I AM NOT DISAPPEARING! This campaign has to be someone who's not going to disappear. I am here!"

Published June 29, 2018

https://panthertimes.com/2018/06/29/raw-interview-of-kenzie-smith-regarding-run-for-oakland-city-council-district-2/

I.G.O.R.B.E.A.T.Z. - The Bay's Best Kept Secret

Many moons back in the 1990's, there were lots of open mics for Bay Area artists to go to almost every night of the week. The Black Box (now the Uptown), Cheri's, Tyrone's, RJ's Lounge, On Broadway, Club Six, Club 101, and most noted, Mingles. Through club gentrification and nightlife violence, others have bowed out or turned a blind eye to up and coming entertainers. There's one open mic still thriving; a hidden gem inside Sweet Fingers on Tuesday nights. It is now known to be the longest running open mic and a staple for up and coming entertainers to perform at. With 25+ years invested, a vital key behind it all can be seen in his DJ booth, getting the artists' tracks ready for them to go on. People may have also seen him around the community at the parks and community events for the kids. He goes by the name of DJ I.G.O.R.B.E.A.T.Z., which is an acronym for, I Grow Off Reality Blessed Everyday Alive Thru Zeal, an acronym given to him by great friend and wordsmith, Akronems of the Writers Block.

I.G.O.R. is a music mailman, because he delivers in so many ways. Since the age of sixteen, I.G.O.R. has deejayed and hosted talent shows, record release parties, block parties, community events and more. His goal was to give up and coming artists an avenue to promote their music. I.G.O.R. linked up with Brian Thomas (a.k.a. "Killa B" the Super Guru), and they founded Baylife Entertainment by combining their companies, Bottom of the Bassment and What Cha Need Graphics. They started off with Brian bringing his artists to perform in I.G.O.R.'s shows, and I.G.O.R. would bring his artists to Brian for custom clothing and flyers. Some of the artists that started coming to Baylife's Open Mics have gone on to make great names for themselves, like Dyson The Singer, Mistah Fab, J Stalin to name a few. Baylife Entertainment is an umbrella, a company of companies. He said, "Through the music, it is a system for artists to invest, create and sell. In the old days, that would be considered a record label." I.G.O.R. evolved into a producer from being a DJ. "My first two turntables were two component sets (you gotta get the book for this story)." At one point, he couldn't rap. He wanted to guide rappers in the studio, and they would disregard his coaching because he wasn't a rapper. "I had to learn how to rap so the rappers I worked with could see my advice works. My friend, Raphael Williams, a.k.a. Mr. Valentine, wrote my first rap, and I still perform it to this day (gotta get the book for this story)."

When you come to Baylife open mic showcases, I.G.O.R. prefers artists not to lip sync. I.G.O.R. expressed his frustration. "New artists don't like my criticism about lip syncing." To me, it shows that they don't practice and take the time to learn the words to their own song. I've seen a lot of great songs ruined with poor stage performance and lip syncin'." He added, "I love teaching the fundamentals to up and coming entertainers. The arts community is growing, and we're taking it to another level. Turning what you love into a business."

Under Baylife Entertainment, they have graphics, recording studios, showcases and events, and an independent radio station with six DJs and radio personalities. The Baylife Team can also be seen at Oakland Unite's Peace at the Park, BBqin' While Black, backpack giveaways, Pop-Ups and other community events. Baylife Radio is another way for independent artists to get their music out to the world. When asked how they came up with an internet radio station, he reflected back to deejaying at KPR1 with a friend, Daniel (a.k.a. Dee-Jiack). Dee-Jiack kept bugging him about being a guest on his radio show. Months later, I.G.O.R. came in to guest DJ the show. The owner of KPR1, Gabe Soloman, heard him DJ and offered him some slots, but he declined to stay working with his friend. Later that year, KPR1 was expanding and had to shut down and relocate to another location. In the process of working at KPR1 and moving the equipment, I.G.O.R. learned how to broadcast through the internet. With the help of DJ Ouma, DJ Teddy B (RIP) and his talented son, DJ TnT, he built Baylife Radio and launched in 2014. "Baylife Radio was only supposed to be temporary until KPR1 was back up and running." It quickly became a full-time project. Baylife Radio is cool because:

1. You can turn it on 24/7 and get great music at www.bayliferadio.com

2. It spotlights up and coming artists while paying homage to the pioneers that paved the way for good music

3. It has a Google app, so you can take it with you anywhere in the world and play it anytime

Through the internet, they reach more people than regional radio. People call in from all over the world. You can find I.G.O.R.B.E.A.T.Z. on Facebook as Richard Gray, @djigorbeatz on Instagram and Twitter, www.bayliferadio.com. Or directly come out to Sweet Fingers open mic on Tuesdays in San Leandro, CA. Also, you can email him your music at djigorbeatz@gmail.com and put in the subject, Attn: For the radio with Song Title and Artist Name.

When asked about the secret to his success, he replied, "My success is an ongoing process. I love seeing the whole team win. I'll do what I have to, to make that happen. That right there is my success!"

Published July 13, 2018

http://www.dopeeramagazine.com/2018/07/13/baylife-entertainment-and-dj-i-g-o-r-b-e-a-t-z-the-bays-best-kept-secret/

We Lead Ours In Oakland

One sunny Saturday in October, I was sitting in the stands at McClymonds High School, watching some boys in cardinal red and gold uniforms tackle another team. I was rooting for the Bay Area Seminoles, a new youth football team, which was in their second year. The youth cheerleaders were doing their thang too! The stands were full of parents and supporters. I didn't remember the last time that I saw so many people show up for a youth football league.

It was like a kid version of The Oakland Raiders' Black Hole. I saw one of the owners and coaches, Lamont Robinson, Jr., walk by and said, "Man, you got a great football league!" He said, "Naw, I got a great organization!"

Bay Area Seminoles is a part of We Lead Ours Organization (WELO, pronounced We-low). It was officially founded in 2010 by three men from Oakland, Dwayne A. Aikens, Jr., Lamont D. Robinson, Jr., and Trestin D. George, who wanted to lead by example and provide for the different needs in the community.

In 2006, they came together to create a program where they could help the children in Oakland. As Lamont said, "The three of us used our brains to make this. We were grassroots in it, and that foundation was the model for our other programs.

They started off with $500 in donations, and they have
never been funded by the federal, state and county.
They get their contributions from community grants,
individual contributions, and corporate sponsors. They
are contracted by the Oakland Unified School District,
servicing nearly 45 school sites in the area of substance
abuse harm reduction. WELO also provides after-school
programming at a variety of schools in Alameda County.

Lamont reflected, "When you see the other parts of the
organization and what we do, you see our footprint.
That looks like Dwayne. Or that looks like Lamont or
Trestin. WELO is the fuel to the engine." They lead
theirs by being more than owners; they are engaged,
and they are out there in the fields with the students.

They are the big brothers in the community. They
provide after-school programs, summer camps, football
and cheer programs, and community
service/internships. The students receive life skill
service learning, community engagement, college prep,
and health and wellness. Their goals are to show the
community that there are more career aspirations other
than being a rapper or an athlete, and to explore
different things in and out of the community.

WELO hosts a mentor/career workshop once a month.
They bring in professionals to show the youth other
career paths. They try to match the students with
someone in that profession so they can get the real
guidance that they need. They prepare them for the life

of being a business owner/entrepreneur. "[The kids say], 'I want to see what the owner life looks like. [Or] I want to be an entrepreneur.' With folks like me, Dwayne and Trestin, to come into our community, coming from poor backgrounds, they can see that it's attainable," Lamont expressed.

At Oakland Unified School District, they work with troubled students who are dealing with life. Many of the students are on probation or have anger issues. WELO team members modify the students' behaviors by motivating them to change their actions and showing them the steps to achieve a goal/dream. Dwayne took that part of the organization to the next level, and they are proud of their after-school programs.

As part of community service through their summer camp and year-round programs, they do backpack giveaways, turkey and toy drives, work with Oakland Parks and Recreation to do cleanups at the parks, Save the Bay, and Creek and Bay Day. Dwayne and Lamont echoed, "We make the kids understand to take care of your home, own community, yourself, and give back." Also, they provide internships and community service to students who need experience, whether it is by working at the snack bar stand, or collecting admission fees to the game, helping out at the summer camp, and mentoring the younger students.

For the Bay Area Seminoles, there are the tricks and the treats. The methods they use are the football and cheer programs to capture the kids, between the ages of 5-14. They check the students' grades to make sure they are eligible to play, and if the students are slipping, they provide tutoring and academic services to get the grades back up.

The treats are parent engagements, family/community support, mentorships, academic support. For the 2018-2019 school year, they will host their first annual ceremony to celebrate the students' academic accomplishments.

They have been recognized by Oakland Mayors, Oakland Raiders, Golden State Warriors, Keep Oakland Beautiful (Dwayne is on the Board), and Waste Management. They are thankful for the support from their partners and other organizations, such as Marshawn Lynch, Lorenzo Alexander, Marcus Peters, Mistah F.A.B., Oakland Fire Department, Oakland Unified School District, and many others.

They have come a long way from where they started, and they plan to leave something in the future. Dwayne said, "There is not enough support in the community, and we aren't in competition with other organizations. We want to collaborate with others who are liked minded. Our passion is what keeps this going." And Lamont added," We love our community. If we're succeeding, it's because the community was behind it and saw what we were doing." Their long-term goal is to expand and work in other cities to give other students in those communities a place to gain exposure and work. And I stand corrected, they are a great organization.

To find out more or support We Lead Ours, you can contact them at https://www.weleadours.org.

 Published July 17, 2018

https://panthertimes.com/2018/07/17/we-lead-ours-in-oakland-program-sets-out-to-turn-troubled-students-to-successful-students/

References:

https://bayareaseminoles.org/

https://www.weleadours.org/

https://www.weleadours.org/about-us.html

Calling Out The Media's Portrayal of Black Victims

There is a history of the media distorting the truth with the portrayal of Black victims when the killer is White. Recently with the killing of Nia Wilson at MacArthur Bart, KTVU found a picture of her holding a gun, which was a cell phone case cover. There were so many pictures to choose from, but they used the one that would make her look threatening. She did not provoke her killer, and the police had to make a statement so people would not lose focus. She was the victim!

Then, the San Francisco Chronicle wrote a story comparing Nia Wilson's life to her killer, John Lee Cowell's life. They wrote it like he did not have a fair chance of growing up and his troubled life led him to that horrible moment. The article read as getting the readers to sympathize with his story and disregard Wilson's life. I took to Twitter and tweeted to the writers of the article, "Why are you trying to humanize the killer? KTVU tried to dehumanize Nia with that one pic from FB, and you are doing an article to sympathize with John Lee Cowell's background. It's so disrespectful to the ladies that didn't deserve this and their family."

They did this with Michael Brown, Trayvon Martin, Emmett Till (until the truth came out last year that he did not do it), and so many others. Then, I thought of a horrible killing of a White girl in the early 1990s, Polly Klaas. A picture of her smiling was always on the news, and celebrities showed their support in finding her. Her story went national to try to see her and her killer. They did not humanize him at all. In fact, he got the death penalty. The killers of Black victims are mostly getting a slap on the wrist, or they are not convicted. Why are their lives valued more than the victims? They say it is not about race, but apparently, it is.

Again, the media can do a convincing job portraying Black people as savages; and will go through anything to tarnish their image before giving them a chance to be innocent. Some celebrities are using their platforms to speak up on the injustices of Black victims and to bring awareness to the social problem. When a Black person is killed, the community has to be ahead and talk about their accomplishments before the media finds one wrong thing; no matter how big or small it may be. It is devastating and causing lack of trust between the community and the media. We know that the press is about viewership and spinning their version of what happened. They will edit what witnesses say to fit their narrative. That is why the community and Black journalists are speaking up and calling them out. At the same time, the community needs more independent media coverage that will reflect what the community is about. The revolution has never been publicized; so it is our duty to do it with social media (drops mic).

Published July 31, 2018

https://panthertimes.com/2018/07/31/calling-out-the-medias-portrayal-of-black-victims/

References:

https://www.washingtonpost.com/news/morning-mix/wp/2018/07/26/critics-say-the-media-makes-innocent-blacks-look-dangerous-heres-their-latest-example/?noredirect=on&utm_term=.7d7686778255

http://www.ktvu.com/news/protest-at-ktvu-over-use-of-inappropriate-nia-wilson-photo

https://www.sfchronicle.com/crime/article/Two-lives-taking-separate-paths-clash-on-BART-13113688.php

https://www.npr.org/sections/codeswitch/2018/07/31/631897758/a-look-back-at-trayvon-martins-death-and-the-movement-it-inspired

https://www.npr.org/sections/thetwo-way/2014/08/11/339592009/people-wonder-if-they-gunned-me-down-what-photo-would-media-use

http://www.blackenterprise.com/black-journalist-nia-wilson/

Jhamel Robinson Blazing Trails in Oakland

Chilling on a sunny day at Lake Merritt, I was able to catch up with Jhamel Robinson. The people walking by us do not know that he blazed the pavements of West Oakland. A true leader who knows how to navigate through the community of Oakland, whether as an owner of The Real Oakland clothing, graphic designer, rapper or a community organizer doing front-line work in the city.

This hometown hero stays innovative and surprising people with his new ideas. A graduate of Oakland Tech High School, he created The Real Oakland clothing from a song that he recorded called "The Real Oakland." A lot of people don't know that he recorded his rap song. "The term came to me, I'm from the real Oakland, and it was in my mind for three weeks. Then my homie, said, 'We should make a song.' I went into the studio to record it and it's on YouTube." With some of his financial aid funding, he created The Real Oakland shirt, with the original colors of black and silver. The Real Oakland brand caught on, especially in the face of gentrification. "For a long time, I just focused on the original design. The other shirts didn't come until later, A Tribe Called Oakland, a design of the old AC Transit paper transfer, and the other ones." All of his shirts reflect the heart and history of Oakland natives and the community.

In addition to his clothing design, he launched a multimedia company called Hippy Genius Media (now called HmtwnHero Branding + Design Specialist) with a photographer Love Quest, which included graphics, photography, and music. He has designed for Dope Era, SoOakland, United Roots, Lorenzo Alexander of the Buffalo Bills, and book covers.

He is a music artist who has released music periodically in the last few years. His biggest claim to fame is a fun song called, "Camera" with CloeyKaboom. They met in high school and started working together after they graduated. He designed her album covers and did some song collaborations with her prior to becoming her full-time manager. He heard her say a line in a song she did with Mistah FAB about "bust it for the camera," and thought that would be a dope song. They collaborated and made "Camera," in 2013. The video takes place at a house party and it is true Oakland in it. Robinson said, "Cloey showed me how much she valued our friendship when she was met with protest from her then record label in regards to releasing the Camera song, which threatened to cancel the release of her album that she had just completed if the song was released. She took that risk for me, but the risk was worth it. I am forever indebted to her for that."

Many do not know that he is one of the organizers of BBQ'n While Black along with Logan McWilliams (recently won East Bay Express Best of the Bay for Best New Cultural Event). For the first one on May 20th, Logan called him and asked him to do a flyer, which featured BBQ Becky and Kenzie Smith from the Lake Merritt incident. It was supposed to be a small event, but the flyer got shared so many times within two hours, that it became bigger. Kenzie Smith contacted Robinson to say, "Let's do it!" Smith used his resources to connect with Oakland councilmembers and community members. To ensure that the event was successful, Robinson secured permits and did everything accordingly so they would not have any issues. Robinson humbly said, "We were expecting like 500 people; 4,000 people showed up. They were calling it the new Festival at the Lake! And, Angela Davis came! That was a sign from the Black Panther Party ancestors that we were making an impact, we were doing what they would've done. And I mean more than Huey, all of them! That meant the most that she showed up."

There was another BBQn' While Black: Poetic Justice Edition on July 1st, which continued the tradition of love and unity in Oakland. There will be a final one for the year in September. The final BBQ'n While Black was supposed to happen in August with a backpack giveaway, but they did not want to conflict with other organizations and people who were already doing theirs. In addition, Robinson expressed frustration that the city is making it harder for him to get permits and adding more regulations. Currently, there are electronic signs saying, "No amplified sounds" or "No double parking." The community is aware of who the signs are referring to.

As the summer is winding down, he recently got a new job with Alternatives In Action to lead an after-school multimedia program at Fremont High School. When he is not busy with organizing an event, designing, managing, he is busy being a father to his daughter. Even though they live in Sacramento due to being priced out of the city, he has to stay in Oakland during the week to be closer to his job. While on the subject of influencing the youth, he referred to the horrible incident with Nia Wilson and her sister at MacArthur Bart Station.

He said, "With what happened to Nia Wilson, I didn't feel like it was the right time to do the BBQ'n While Black event. My niece was friends with her, so I felt that I needed to be there for her and her close-knit friends as somewhat a young elder of the community. The community is hurting and it is my duty to heal the community. Someone has to step up and show these kids the right way to grieve. They are drinking and smoking to numb their pain, and aren't able to express themselves in a positive light. Fifteen years ago, I was them and I can identify with them. Kids can see when you're full of shit. They need someone to talk to and get real advice." He wants to be an example to the kids and show them that they can be successful. He hopes that they will make it and come back to show others how to make it. As for the violence happening, he wants the community to know that if they are going to protest against a murder by a White person, they need to protest against the violence by Blacks. Violence is violence; and people should not be picking and choosing when and what to protest.

So much wisdom from this young man who has a birthday coming up. He has grown in so many ways since the launch of The Real Oakland and has always attended community events. He published a poetry book, *Layers Of An Imperfect Soul*, earlier this year, and he stays expanding. Nothing seems to be one thing with him; and he never knows where his path will lead him. When asked what's next for him, Robinson concluded, "Every good thing that happens [to me] is on accident."

Published August 3, 2018

http://www.dopeeramagazine.com/2018/08/03/jhamel-robinson-blazing-trails-in-oakland/

Black Literary Collective at Youth Uprising

What is the Black Literary Collective? How did you come up with the concept?

The Black Literary Collective (BLC) is a group of extremely diverse and talented black authors, who are passionate about serving the community through their literary and community work. The idea for the BLC came to me after doing a number of events in schools and community spaces for my book *Black Boy Poems*. Seeing young people respond with so much excitement to an author who comes from their same context, and seeing literary works that feature their context, made me want to find ways to expand that impact. I'm a product of the colonial public school system, and [I] know what it's like to be disengaged from the curriculum due to the lack of black literature and authors, and my story never being told. I knew we could create a group of powerful brothers and sisters who could make sure that this would not be the reality of students in schools today.

You have ten authors. How did you choose your writers? What do they represent in the collective?

We have ten authors as of now, and eventually will expand to include more. The six brothers and four sisters who are the founding members of the collective are tremendous people. Some of the best folks I could ever want to be connected to and work with. Many of them I was lucky to consider friends before starting the collective, and a few I met during book events. They are all highly respected by the community. They also represent different lived experiences and genres of work. I wanted to create a cross section of the black experience so that the community could really see the beauty of who we are in the work that is represented. I was trying to have an equal balance between men and women; but I fell short on that for now. We have children's books, memoirs, poets, fiction writers, emotional intelligence/self-development and revolutionary literature represented in our collective. We have college graduates and folks who became victims of the prison industrial complex. We also have a member that fiercely represents our disabled community. It wouldn't be a true representation of our African diaspora without featuring at least one member from the African continent, we are blessed to have an incredible author from East Africa on our roster. It is a must that our people can see powerful representations of the beautiful diversity that makes us who we are.

You have a launch event on September 15th at Youth Uprising. What do you want people to take away from the event?

The goal of the launch event is to introduce the collective to the community. We have been doing work in the schools and the communities, but it is time to expand what we're able to do for the community. We'll be highlighting what we offer as a collective. Author's talks, forums, workshops, collaborative programs, curriculum development, trainings and professional development. Folks in attendance will learn about the collective, and we'll start scheduling dates for the collective to begin working with various organizations. We will have some fun but also get to work.

If people cannot attend, how can they get in touch with you?

If folks want to learn more about the collective, they can reach out here: blacklitcollective@gmail.com

Or visit us at: www.blacklitcollective.com

We all can serve the people in our own ways. I believe the BLC is a great first step in interrupting curriculum that does not prioritize the black experience in classroom settings. We need the help and support of the community to make sure that our young folks receive a proper revolutionary educational foundation, so that they can be the agents of change our communities need.

Published September 13, 2018

https://panthertimes.com/2018/09/13/black-literary-collective-launches-at-youth-uprising/

Oakland Celebrates Weekend of Black Liberation and Calls for Unity with All Communities

October 15, 1966, the Black Panther Party was born in Oakland, CA. October 13 and 14, 2018, we were celebrating a movement that changed everyone's lives, especially in Oakland. It is the celebration that we need, to slap gentrification in the face, and let it be known that the descendants of the party are still here. Many may not be able to afford living here, but we gathered in honor of Huey Newton. Bobby Seale, Lil Bobby Hutton, Elbert "Big Man" Howard, and so many more.

Life Is Living by Youth Speaks kicked off its annual celebration at De Fremery Park, also known as, Lil Bobby Hutton Park. With performances from youth groups, a tribute to Aretha Franklin, and so many more, it was the creative outlet that the community needed. The park was packed with many community members and organizations that reflect what the Black Panther Party represented. There were young people registering people to vote for the mid-term elections. One man was just released from probation, and he registered right there as he rode in. To witness that moment was something to document.

Sunday's 52nd Anniversary in downtown Oakland had the messages that we needed to keep that spirit alive. Hosted by Gina Madrid and Saturu Ned, with various speakers from Kenzie Smith, Cat Brooks, Ashara

Ekundayo, and performers such as Ras Ceylon, Kev Choice, Jennifer Johns, Khafre Jay, and others, the messages were heard loud and clear. The city is pushing us out, and it is different from when the Black Panther Party started. It is strategic to organize and hit the polls. The celebration was in the middle of the all high rise developments, and a few blocks from the Oakland Police Department. It was the epitome of why the Party was established. As Saturu Ned said, "We had determination, and we were serving the community." With so many of us working independently or with our own organizations in the community, we are doing what the Panthers would be doing. We are the children and nieces/nephews of the original members, and we were instilled to give back and be the impact.

Register to vote and be the change you want to see. Just like in 1972, when Bobby Seale and Elaine Brown were running for office, the people running for office are local community members who are tired of the system, and tired of not seeing anything done in City Hall. There are so many people doing things grassroots that they do not always have the financial capital to do what they do, yet are making it happen. "A local organization became a global movement," Saturu Ned reminded us. We have to come together to save our schools, neighborhoods, give each other skills so we can employ ourselves. If the Black Panthers were able to do their survival programs, then we should keep providing survival programs. There are way too many resources for us to tap into, especially with the power of the internet. As the theme said for the rally, All Power to the People!

 Published October 19, 2018

https://panthertimes.com/2018/10/19/oakland-celebrates-weekend-of-black-liberation-and-calls-for-unity-with-all-communities/